PREPARING YOUR CHILD
FOR ACADEMIC SUCCESS

Nobody Told Me About
Sensory Development

PREPARING YOUR CHILD FOR ACADEMIC SUCCESS

Newborn to Age Six

Enjoyable Practical Tools
That Motivate Children to Learn at a Higher Level

For Parents, Grandparents, and Caregivers

Plus:
- Academic Success Tips for the Elementary Child
- Keeping Your Adolescent Focused – Middle / High School and College Age

Terri Hadley

Cover design by Caitlin B. Alexander
Interior design by Sarah Lahay

Paperback: 979-8-9863679-0-3
Ebook: 979-8-9863679-1-0

1st Edition, Revised January 2024
Printed in the United States of America

terbeartwin2@cox.net

DEDICATION

To my two children, whom I am so proud of for your work ethics, good hearts, and achievements. Continue to achieve your every dream.

To my twin granddaughters, who are so beautiful. Because of this knowledge in sensory development, I can be a confident grandparent in helping prepare you for academic success. I look forward to watching you both grow and be successful women.

CONTENTS

Introduction

This book will teach parents, grandparents, or caregivers to understand how to help the infant's and child's senses develop to an age appropriate or higher level in preparation for academic success. We will explore the interest period of the infant and child, as well as the best developmental toys appropriate for enhancement of the senses at each age. I will explain the proper use of these toys. In addition, I will describe how to enhance tracking and speed for reading, and how to improve concentration or attention span. A ball skills program for developing gross motor skills, focusing, tracking, and following directions will also be discussed.

As an added bonus, I will give academic success tips for the elementary child, which may also help a child labeled with a mild to moderate learning disability, such as dyslexia, or the disability Attention Deficit Hyperactivity Disorder (ADHD) overcome obstacles in learning. In addition, Erikson's Psychosocial Stages for a healthy personality from birth through the elementary years will be explained. Finally, I will recommend tips for keeping your adolescent focused through the college years.

This book is merely a guideline in preparation for academic success and the prevention of many learning disabilities. Every child is unique. What works for one child may not work for another in developing the senses. It is important to determine the interest of the infant or child, which will be discussed in Chapter 2. Please review each age group as your child attains that age.

I wrote this book because when I tutored elementary students, I noticed they were unnecessarily lacking important developmental steps. When I lectured, parents said they wished there was a class on Sensory Development for Academic Success. For that reason, I wanted to give parents, grandparents, and caregivers the confidence in helping to raise an independent, confident, successful, and productive child.

When I began studying sensory development, I was 29 years old and decided to enter a vision training program to help my eyes coordinate together and focus better. I have strabismus (a lazy eye) that was prominent from birth. Shortly after I began reading pamphlets on Attention Deficit Disorder (ADD) and ADHD symptoms in children, I realized these symptoms were the same as mine. Yet, these children did not have a lazy eye. Simply put, they were lacking vision development. I walked into my optometrist's office one day and said, "Oh my gosh, many of these children labeled ADD and ADHD really don't have it. They are deficient in vision development because they missed developmental steps." My developmental optometrist replied, "I can't believe you figured th s out." I also realized many children labeled with dyslexia were also lacking vision skills because they were missing vital developmental steps. Then, I recognized something else. My own two children were missing vital developmental steps in preparation for school success. At that time, my children were three and four years of age, and I did not know about sensory development in preparing them academically.

In this book I hope to provide school preparation techniques, developmental toy suggestions for higher learning, and methods to prevent the development of many learning disabilities. Some of the goals I have for you are as follows:

1. Shop at a toy store of your choice, and choose the correct toy to enhance or develop your child's senses.

2. Understand the age appropriate interest period so you and your child will not bypass this developmental milestone.

3. Remember to give your child ample opportunities to play with some of the sensory toys.

4. Gain knowledge in helping your child have self-worth, confidence, independence, and success.

Vocabulary

TERMS / CONCEPTS

- Categorization
- Cause and Effect
- Descriptive Writing Technique
- Directionality
- Fine Motor Skills
- Habituated
- Interest of the Infant
- Interest Period
- Large Motor Skills
- Object Permanence
- Sensory Integration Technique (Multisensory Learning)
- Self-reflection
- Self-reliance

- Sequencing
- Sorting by Color or Shape
- The Three
- Transfer Technique

NOTE: These terms and concepts are used throughout the text and are identified in **BOLD** print.

CHAPTER 1

Arrangement and Safety of the Room

ARRANGEMENT AND SAFETY OF THE ROOM

Before I begin discussing toys that enhance the development of the senses, I need to explain the arrangement and safety of the room. If you have not read the introduction to this book, I would like to ask that you do so in order for you to better understand the importance of why and what I am teaching.

In my evaluation, I have discovered the book *Montessori from the Start: The Child at Home, from Birth to Age Three*[1] explains many areas on how to arrange the room properly for the infant to see and move safely.

- The ability of an infant to move and explore is very important because he/she may become bored or depressed if restrained.

- Keep blankets, toys or stuffed animals out of the sleeping area. The Halo SleepSack may be used in lieu of blankets to keep the infant safe and allow him/her to move (see Swaddling, Pacifiers, and Tummy Time).

- For safety reasons, place a gate in the doorway so when the infant begins to scoot, he/she stays in the room.

- Bolt windows closed if windows are not at a safe height.

- Keep cords away and out of reach of the infant.

- Place a large (two to three feet) square mirror made of safety glass by the infant's bed so the baby can see himself or herself and their room. The mirror should be secured safely to the wall so the infant cannot pull it off or so it doesn't fall.

- Soothing colors and simple patterns on the wall are best. Too many busy patterns could over stimulate the infant.

- One rattle can be placed in a wicker or safety-type basket.

- At six months, three toys can be placed in the wicker basket. A suggestion would be a rattle, ball, and wooden ring or other toys of interest to the infant.

SWADDLING, PACIFIERS, AND TUMMY TIME

 Don't bundle or tuck the infant so tight with blankets or swaddling that he/she cannot move. Also, this can over stimulate the baby before sleep.

Many parents use the Halo SleepSack for their newborn baby. One is called Halo SleepSack Swaddle for the newborn. Using this sack allows the infant to move and place his/her arms outside of the sack. This sack also helps to prevent Sudden Infant Death Syndrome (SIDS). Don't place heavy clothing under the SleepSack. This could overheat the infant. A lightweight sleeper or, in summertime, a onesie may suffice. There are also a variety of Halo SleepSacks for older infants.

NOTE: As the infant begins to roll (this can be as early as two months), he/she should not be swaddled due to an increase risk of SIDS when the baby tries to move. If you are using the Halo SleepSack Swaddle for the newborn, I suggest placing the infant's arms outside the sack very early on. Follow the directions for the Halo SleepSack Swaddle. You can purchase the Halo SleepSack at www.halosleep.com.

 Pacifiers prevent the infant from babbling; consequently, the baby has difficulty producing sound.[2] Some articles say that there may be speech and language delays from using pacifiers.[3] Also, there is some evidence that middle ear infections can occur, which can cause hearing loss. However, other articles say infants can use a pacifier at nap or sleep time to help prevent SIDS.[4] Some babies may need the pacifier to help with the development of sucking such as a preemie baby. Ask your doctor cr nurse.

For an older infant and if you are using a pacifier during the day, instead of putting the pacifier in the baby's mouth, you might want to try giving a toy of interest to the infant instead. My own two children did not like pacifiers. They would spit them out.

Therefore, I did not force the pacifier upon them. Additionally, I am grateful I did not have the worry of weening them off pacifiers. Yet, you as a parent have to decide what is best for your infant in determining the use of pacifiers.

- Allow some time for the infant to lay on his/her stomach during waking time so the baby can practice lifting his/her head.[5]

- When dressing an infant, dress him or her in the exact order every time.[6] See Chapter 3 for the importance of sequencing.

For new parent(s), having a newborn can be overwhelming, exhausting and can lead to miscommunication due to the extra workload. I have come across this issue many times and hope this suggestion will clarify communication. Create a list as to which parent will do what chore. For example, who will wash bottles, cook, clean, or do laundry? Will you both take turns feeding the baby and changing diapers? Both parents may need to take a 45-minute break in the evening to refresh themselves. If you are a single parent, I suggest having a grandparent, relative, or friend give you a break a couple of times a week. If they are will'ng to help out with laundry or cooking, that would be helpful as well. I truly hope you will take the time to rest and communicate.

NOTES

1   Lillard, P. P., & Jessen, L. L. (2003). *Montessori from the Start*. New York: Schocken Books (pp 32–33).

2   Lillard, P. P., & Jessen, L. L. (2003). *Montessori from the Start*. New York: Schocken Books (pp 165)

3   Jones, S. (January 8, 2015). *Does Sucking on a Pacifier Harm Speech Development?* - www.nspt4kids.com

4   Mayo Clinic Staff. (July 22, 2017). *Pacifiers: Are They Good for Your Baby?* - www.mayoclinic.org

5   Lillard, P. P., & Jessen, L. L. (2003). *Montessori from the Start*. New York: Schocken Books (pp 75)

6   Lillard, P. P., & Jessen, L. L. (2003). *Montessori from the Start*. New York: Schocken Books (pp 147–148)

CHAPTER 2

Toys — Birth to 12 Months

TOYS – BIRTH TO 12 MONTHS

As I begin to discuss the infant's first toy, I want to point out that I have spent hours in toy stores exploring, analyzing, and manipulating toys that I believe enhance the senses of the child. Since I've been through a Vision Training program, it is easier for me to determine in one to two weeks whether the toy will enhance the senses or hinder the development of the senses. Additionally, I have spent hours observing children manipulating these toys in determining their interests. Parental feedback has helped my decision in choosing toys, as has using these many toys in tutoring young elementary students. Most of the toys I have chosen are from the store Lakeshore Learning; Discovery Toys; www.montessorioutlet.com; Melissa and Doug; and Target Stores, or Walmart.

As an added bonus, I will be explaining Erik Erikson's Psychosocial Stages at each age group. Erikson's Psychosocial Stages are divided into eight age groups. Each stage helps with personality development in creating a strong sense of self. Parents and teachers can influence a strong sense of self. The stage could end in a positive or negative result. Of course, we want our children to achieve each age group with a positive result. If the child does not get through the stage with a positive result, it can be remediated through life experiences. There will be suggestions for solutions on how to achieve each stage positively from birth to the elementary child.

Erik Erikson's Stage 1[1,2] **— Hope: Trust versus Mistrust, 0 to 1-1/2 years.**
The significant person such as mother or caregiver should meet the basic needs of the infant. Listen to the cues of the infant. Is the baby hungry, or wet? Does the baby need to be comforted? The infant needs to know he/she can depend on you and to feel loved.

DETERMINING THE INTEREST OF THE INFANT

In determining the readiness or **interest of the infant** for a toy and future toys, notice whether the baby is staring at the toy or avoiding it. If the infant is staring at the toy, he/she is interested or ready. If the infant is avoiding looking at the toy, he/she is not interested or not ready. The toy may be too detailed. Therefore, change the toy to see if the baby is staring at it with readiness.

FIRST TOYS

Mobiles are first toys. Within a couple of weeks after birth one can hang a flat black and white mobile made of geometric shapes on large index cards so the infant can see the flat sides of the mobile (this is the first mobile).[3] You can make this yourself. There is also a link for instructions on homemade mobiles (https://www.homedit.com/how-to-make-a-baby-mobile/). Hang the mobile about 10 to 15 inches from the eyes, but out of reach of the infant. For safety reasons, make sure the mobile pieces cannot fall on the infant. It is usually easier for a newborn infant to focus on black and white first. The next mobile in two weeks should include more detail, but I still suggest black and white such as the *Art Cards for Baby* by Wee Gallery. I like the Original Collection or the Farm Collection. Parental feedback suggests babies do like these cards. You can purchase the Kikkerland Hanging Display Photo Hanger to hang the geometric shapes and cards from Amazon. The art cards can also be purchased from Wee Gallery.

It is always best to present a toy with less detail to an infant or child to begin with, and then present a more detailed toy later. The mobiles aid the infant in beginning to track and focus on an object. The black and white also helps the infant begin to develop perception of color and depth. Target stores also carry a gray and white *Crib Mobile Two by Two* made by Cloud Island that hangs on the crib for a beginning mobile.

Determine the **interest of the infant**. If the infant does not look at the handmade geometric shapes, then try the gray and white crib mobile from Target or the *Art Cards for Baby* to see if the infant is looking at them and therefore interested. Make sure mobiles swing slowly so the infant can track. A little later (about two to four weeks) color mobiles can be used. Our world is made up of colors and shapes so it is important for the infant to begin noticing these from the beginning. You may like the other crib mobiles at Target that begin to use color for the infant as well. Alternating the mobile every two weeks helps development and keeps the infant interested. Mobiles are used for three months (although mobiles can be hung longer, even as long as one year of age).

Mobiles after four weeks may be in **sequencing** order. This includes a mobile of primary colors, then a mobile of gradations in the same color, and a mobile made of wood in pastel colors. (You can also refer to a suggestion on **sequencing** of mobiles from the book *Montessori from the Start*). Also, Skyflight Mobiles (www.hangingmobilegallery. com) sells a *Butterfly Combo Mobile* that my twin grandchildren have loved from about 10 weeks old. They still enjoy this mobile at nine months of age. The reason I chose this mobile is for the vivid colors, the different distances of the butterflies for the infant to focus and track, and the differences in detail of each butterfly. I cannot stress this mobile enough for enhancing vision development in focusing, tracking, and noticing the differences in detail. The infant may be ready to focus on this mobile before two months of age. Again, check for readiness.

Another toy you can display for the infant usually within a few weeks after birth is called the *Manhattan Toy Wimmer-Ferguson Learning Cube Multisensory Soft Baby Activity Toy*. This helps the infant begin to recognize shapes and patterns. Also, the black and white contrast helps the infant focus, which is usually appeasing to the infant. This Manhattan Toy Learning Cube should be displayed 10 to 15 inches away from the infant. One can place this toy out for tummy time as well. I encourage you to add this important first toy to your collection. It helps the infant learn how to use its senses. Available on Amazon.

Rattles are first toys too. I want to point out the first set of rattles I discovered for easy grasping is called *Links* or *Boomerings*. These can be purchased from a Discovery Toys representative or Amazon. A ring can be given to the infant within two weeks after birth or when the baby can grasp your finger (some infants may not be ready). Once the infant can grasp one link easily, you can add two links for the baby to grasp. The baby can now hear the links clinking together. Change the color of the link periodically so the infant can see the variety of colors. The *Links* are an important beginning for sensory development. One such study *Postural Variability and Sensorimotor Development in Infancy* states, "Visual attention combined with active experiences contacting the object advances the development of reaching more than passive interactions or only visualizing the object."[4]

These sensory books are also good as first books to enable infants to focus. Some are called *Look. Look!*, and *Look at the Animals*, and other infant books by Peter Linenthal. In the first month of life the infant may be interested in viewing these books as the parent turns each page. Another interesting book is called *Goodnight Moon* by Margaret Wise Brown. This colorful book begins with daytime brightness and ends with nighttime dimness. All of these sensory books can be purchased from Amazon.

Beginning at birth, sing children's songs such as "Twinkle, Twinkle, Little Star." This enhances auditory processing, and later on will help with reading.[5]

THREE TO SIX MONTHS TOYS

At approximately three months (or maybe earlier depending on the infant), rattles or simple objects such as the Kringelring Clutching Toy (wooden ring) from HABA can now be hung using elastic so the infant can reach and begin to grab or bat at them.[6] This helps develop depth perception and enables the baby to hear sounds from the rattles. Thus, the infant is using vision, auditory, and tactile senses simultaneously. Make sure the elastic cannot fall off from where you secured it. Also, make sure rattles are safe for the baby, such as not being sharp, or that small parts cannot fall off the rattle easily. Change a rattle about every week or two depending on the **interest of the infant**. See a baby catalog for rattles, or Discovery Toys catalog, Target, Walmart or HABA. I like the HABA clutching toys or rattles because they are made of quality wood. The book *Montessori from the Start* emphasizes using wood toys rather than plastic or metal because wood toys show grains and have different smells depending on the type of wood. Wood toys also have different sounds if clanged together. The book *Montessori from the Start* also gives some important logical progression of rattles. A baby usually begins to play with rattles between three and six months.

Baby Activity Mats are great for the infant to bat and reach at different objects as well as for learning cause and effect. These *Activity Mats* that already come with hanging toys can be used in lieu of hanging rattles from elastic if you are not comfortable hanging toys from elastic. I used this toy for the grandtwins instead. I like the mats that cross at the top because the toys hang in different areas and distances for the baby's eyes to view. This can help develop the peripheral vision from the different areas, as well as the central vision viewing the top toy. *Baby Activity Mats* can be purchased from Walmart or Target.

At this age, you can begin alternating an age appropriate toy every three days to a week depending on the **interest of the infant**. If the infant is still playing with the toy given him or her at three days, do not give the baby another toy. He/she is still interested in the toy and therefore learning. However, if the infant is ignoring the toy at three days, then introduce another toy because he/she has **habituated** or become bored with that toy. Thus, the infant is no longer stimulated and learning. You can reintroduce the toy at a later time to re-stimulate learning because the infant will be at a new developmental level. This is called alternating the toys, and also determines the **interest of the infant**. I suggest only placing one or two toys out at a time. If one places a lot of toys out at once, the infant can become overwhelmed and may not play with them.

NOTE: Some babies may need a different toy every day to keep them from habituating.

BEFORE THE INFANT BEGINS TO CRAWL TOYS

 You can use a basket or similar object to place safe items in, such as plastic measuring cups or spoons from your kitchen, etc. Only place three items in the basket. Later, you can add four or five items to the basket. Using kitchen items, then changing items to another category such as transportation items (a car, a train, and a plane) in a week or two already is teaching **categorization**. Make sure all items are safe for the infant to play with.

 Manhattan Toy's *Skwish Classic* is a toy that is multidimensional. This toy can be hung first. When the baby sits, he/she can then play with the toy. This can be purchased at www. amazon.com.

Colorpillar Sorting Mat for ages six months +. I highly recommend having this in your toy collection. Some parents have said they put this toy out as early as five months old (parental supervision, please). The *Colorpillar Sorting Mat* encourages scooting, crawling, and other physical activity. It consists of 18 different manipulatives in various materials, shapes, textures (soft and hard), and colors. You can also place the baby's favorite toy to scoot to on this mat. The manipulatives included in the *Colorpillar* stimulate tactile, smell, and vision senses. The *Colorpillar* also introduces the infant to the concept of **sorting by color or shape**. When older, the child will most likely spend hours sorting different items. The *Colorpillar Sorting Mat* is available at Lakeshore Learning.

 When the baby sits up, a toy called the *Object Permanence Box w/ Tray* may be used. Test the **interest of the infant** for readiness which is around eight months. The *Object Permanence Box w/ Tray* develops eye-hand coordination. It also develops the concept of **object permanence**— meaning an object can disappear and still be present. You can order this toy from www.montessorioutlet.com. Melissa and Doug or HABA toys may also carry this item. Next, the baby can use a box called the *Shape Sorting Cube Classic Toy* by Melissa and Doug, or something similar can be purchased at Walmart. This toy fosters **fine motor skills** (finger development), color and shape recognition, and visualization. Some of the sorting cubes are made for 18 months, but infants as early as 10 months will play with this type of toy with parental supervision. This is an important skill. There is also a sorting cube by Fisher-Price called *Baby's First Blocks Shape Sorting Toy* —ages six months + (Shop. mattel.com).

 You can introduce stacking toys at about nine months to one year of age. Again, test the **interest of the infant** for readiness. An excellent stacking toy is called the *MEASURE UP! CUPS Stack & Learn*. This can be purchased at Discovery Toys. I suggest first you place the largest half of the stacking cups in front of the infant and snow him/her how to stack them. Once the baby can stack the largest half (this may take a week or two), then place the smaller half of the stacking cups in front of the infant and show him/her. Finally, as the baby can stack the larger and smaller halves separately, then place all of the stacking cups in front of the infant to stack and show him or her. Some infants at 10 months old can stack all the measuring cups. Other infants may not be ready to do this until after one year of age. The brain is now discriminating the differing sizes through touch and sight using the tactile and vision senses.

One of the toys I like for the stroller is called the *Try-Angle*. This toy stimulates auditory and visual skills, and teaches **cause and effect**. You can also place this toy out during tummy time, or when the infant begins to sit. The *Try-Angle* toy can be purchased from a Discovery Toys representative or Amazon.

Mobiles, rattles, household items, wooden toys made of shapes, *Skwish*, the *Colorpillar*, and measuring cups are some of my favorite toys for developing the senses.

NOTE: If the infant is crawling toward an object or path that's undesirable, step in front of him or her to change the baby's direction. Do not pick the infant up so he/she does not rely on you. This fosters **self-reliance.**

NOTES

1   Wikipedia. (April 12, 2020). *Erikson's Stages of Psychosocial Development* - en.m.wikipedia.org

2   McLeod, Saul. (July 2, 2017). *Erik Erikson's Stages of Psychosocial Development* - www.simplypsychology.org

3   Lillard, P. P., & Jessen, L. L. (2003). *Montessori from the Start*. New York: Schocken Books (pp 44)

4   Dusing, Stacey C. (March 29 2016). *Postural Variability and Sensorimotor Development In Infancy - Developmental Medicine and Child Neurology* - www.onlinelibrary.wiley.com

5   Collins, Anita, & Adoniou, Misty. (November 9, 2018). *Music Can Help Young Children With Reading. This Is How.* www.weforum.org

6   Lillard, P. P., & Jessen, L. L. (2003). *Montessori from the Start*. New York: Schocken Books (pp 45)

CHAPTER 3

12 Months to Two Years

12 MONTHS TO TWO YEARS

At this age you can give your child a variety of stacking toys called *Stack and Nest Toys* (see samples at www.melissaanddoug.com) and any toys incorporating shapes such as simple building blocks as age appropriate. Simple building blocks enhance creativity and visualization. Visualization will help children later on for math and language. Again, you can place one or two toys in front of the child to determine the interest. Additionally, I now suggest you place age appropriate toys on shelves, not in toy boxes. Make sure the shelf is secure and cannot fall on the infant or toddler. Begin rotating the toys on the shelves every week or two to re-stimulate the child to notice the toys. The child will usually choose a toy of his or her interest to manipulate.

Let's Go Fishing! Playset — 12 months +. I am very impressed with this toy to enhance depth perception, eye-hand coordination and fine motor skills for pencil holding. The *Let's Go Fishing! Playset* can be purchased at Lakeshore Learning.

Spike The Fine Motor Hedgehog — 18 months +. Fine motor skills and counting. Several toys in Chapter 3 enhance fine motor skills. If developed early, this may alleviate the frustration of pencil holding in preschool and early elementary school. Don't be alarmed if your child is not ready for this toy. Try again in a couple of weeks. The *Spike Hedgehog* by Learning Resources can be purchased at Amazon.

MiniSpinny. An excellent toy for finger control. At about 12 months you can begin showing your toddler how to spin this toy. Hold the toy vertical and spin the three prongs for the toddler. Once the toddler has seen you do this several times (this may take days or weeks), the toddler should be able to spin the prongs himself/herself while you hold the toy vertically. A couple of weeks later, you can show the child horizontally how to spin the toy. Make sure when placing the toy horizontally the prongs spin left to right for the child as in reading. Eventually, the toddler should be able to hold the *MiniSpinny* on his/her own and spin the toy vertically or horizontally. The *MiniSpinny* can be purchased at Amazon.

Spark. Create. Imagine. Wooden Animal Blocks includes bright colored blocks that attract children to play with this toy. Children can stack and create using their imagination. Cause and effect from stacking,[1] creativity and visualization are enhanced. If the child acts frustrated when the stacking blocks fall, I suggest saying "Ooh" and giving a little chuckle so the child laughs along with you. Then say, "Let's try again." This demonstrates to the child stacking is fun. *Spark. Create. Imagine. Wooden Animal Blocks* can be purchased at Walmart.

Shape Sorting Turtle — 12 months +. Sorting, shape recognition, eye-hand coordination.
The *Shape Sorting Turtle* or *Wooden Shape Sorter* can be purchased at Lakeshore Learning.

Rollipop Advanced — 9 months + (manufacturer). However, I recommend 12 months +. I suggest placing this toy against a wall due to its light weight. An excellent toy for eye tracking a ball. Later on eye tracking is used for reading. The Rollipop Advanced can be purchased at Target, Amazon, and other online retailers.

Archway Water Table by Step2 is an excellent water toy that enhances fine motor skills and teaches cause and effect. This toy is for ages one and a half on up, and I suggest playing through the early elementary years if children are interested. (This can be purchased at Costco, Walmart and many other places. Prices vary, so please shop for the best deal. I purchased mine at Costco.) I am a proponent for cause and effect n the Sciences. In the article "Sensory Science: Connecting Children's Science Learning to Their Sensory Play,"[2] it discusses sensory science activities and gives questions for sensory play and scientific thinking. Questions such as "What objects float and what objects sink in water?" and "What happens when I add blocks to my boat?"

DRESS AND SEQUENCING

At 12 months to two years a child is **interested** in dressing himself or herself. He/she may be able to dress himself or herself at 14 months. When you dress the infant or child, dress him or her slowly and in the exact order every time. For example, put the pants on first with the right pant leg, then the left pant leg; then the top with the right sleeve and left sleeve. And finally, the right bootie and then the left bootie. This begins to teach **sequencing** which helps the child to think in a logical organized order. **Sequencing** will later on be used by the child in reading as in knowing the beginning, middle, and ending of a story.

You can give the child two choices of dress, not three, for him/her to choose from. If the child cannot make a decision, then choose for him/her. Don't allow children to debate; because, otherwise clothes may become too important to them.[3]

The child should be able to brush or comb hair at two years.

TODDLER — INTEREST PERIOD

This is the period where the child is most interested in work and begins at about 18 months, which I call the **Interest Period**. Montessori calls this type of **interest period** Practical Life. Erik Erikson's stage defines it as interest for self-sufficiency. This is a very important age to begin chores because of the interest of the toddler in chores. If you wait till age four to teach a child to pick up toys or do chores, then the child will usually resist because he/she missed the **interest period**. Examples of work at this age are sweeping, pouring water into pitchers, setting the table, folding laundry, etc., anything to do with chores. This builds the finger skills called **fine motor** and **sequencing**.

Erik Erikson's Stage 2 — Will: Autonomy versus Shame — Ages 1-1/2 to 3.

This stage encourages self-sufficiency such as being able to dress oneself. The child has the sense "I can do it myself." This helps the child to be able to handle problems on his/her own. Make sure the child is interested in dressing him/herself so you don't demand too soon. If you ridicule a child, he/she may not dress himself or herself, and shame or doubt could occur.

The book *Montessori from the Start* does an excellent job of explaining the organization of cupboards for the child to learn to **categorize** and **sequence**.[4]

Give the child his or her own cupboard with utensils in proper order. If possible have three shelves. The first shelf for placemat, napkins, and a basket of six identical sets of spoons and forks. They should be placed back in the cupboard in this **exact** order after playing with them. You will most likely have to show the child two or three times how to do this correctly.

The second shelf can consist of six identical bowls and six identical salad plates.

Finally, on the bottom shelf, you can place two small glass pitchers (transparent) and eight small glasses made of glass. The reason for glass is to teach the child to develop more control and to learn to be careful. It also teaches the child to trust himself/herself. (Many toddlers may not be ready for this glass exercise until three to four years of age.) You can purchase these glass items at www.montessoriservices.com. The glass at Montessori Services is a type of glass that if it breaks it does not break into sharp pieces. Teach the child to carry the glass to the table with two hands. If a spill occurs, or there is broken glass, show the child how to clean up so he is able to do this himself/herself. I once saw a child in a Montessori classroom drop a glass. It shattered into un-sharp pieces because of the tempered glass. The child, who was only about three and a half years old, actually cleaned up the glass pieces by sweeping them into a dust pan. At 20 to 24 months a child can usually pour his or her own drink (age varies depending on finger control).

NOTE: Make sure the table height is not too high for the child's work or play. A table too high or close to the child's eyes can affect the child's visual focusing. The height should be at about the belly button. You can also purchase children's chairs and tables at different heights. If you see the child laying his/her head down or eyes too close while coloring or other art work, help him/her to sit back up in the chair. Make sure the feet are on the ground also. One chair I discovered that is adjustable and can be brought to the dinner table is called the Stokke Tripp Trapp High Chair. It has a place to put the toddler's feet that adjusts as the child grows. This can be used from toddler even through the early elementary years. I tutored a kindergartener who did her school work at the dinner table and used the Stokke Tripp Trapp chair. The chair is pricey, but you may be able to purchase it on Amazon for less money. Visit www.stokke.com or www.amazon.com.

When you clean the table in front of the child, wipe from left to right, top to bottom as in reading a book.

If a child is using a broom for his/her Practical Life activity and begins to swing the broom, take the broom away until another day. The broom is a tool for a purpose. Give the child another activity instead.

BUILDING CONCENTRATION

Avoid interrupting the child while he/she is playing with the educational toys. The child needs to concentrate or focus and do the activity for himself/herself, not others, meaning intrinsic motivation.[5] Interrupting to praise the child will break his or her concentration, and may cause him or her to believe the work is meant to please his/her parents. We want the child to develop concentration at this stage. You can, however, praise the child after the activity.

ROUTINE

Routine and order are important in the first three years. For example, the child should have the same mealtime, bath time, and bedtime every day. As the child is able to clean his/her room, it is suggested that he/she clean it at the same time every day.

LANGUAGE DEVELOPMENT, EXPLORATION AND MORE

From *Montessori from the Start*,[6] paraphrasing:

Begin to hold the child's hand in public places when toddler begins to walk for safety reasons. If you wait until two or three years of age, this could turn into a power struggle of resistance.

If a child becomes silly or destructive, this means tne child is tired or bored and can no longer focus. A young child cannot tell you this at this age. You need to redirect the child to another activity, or perhaps place him down for a nap.

For language development, at about 12 months (age varies) begin teaching your infant object items such as, "this is Grandma's ring." Or, "this is your hair." Or, 'this is a clock." This may need to be taught over and over again for a while (perhaps two to three weeks). Then once are confident he/she knows what these items are, begin asking the infant questions such as, "Where's Grandma's ring,"

"Where's the clock," "Where's your hair?" etc. The infant will usually point to the ring, or clock, or his/her hair. Now that your infant can point to the item, begin asking your child "What is this?" It is important to begin asking, "What is this?" as soon as possible to help the child verbalize.

Exploration of nature for the child begins at about 18 months. You can take your child, for example, to the park or beach and follow behind. For safety reasons, stay very close within visual distance. Your toddler can learn a lot about his or her world through exploration. This will also stimulate the child's senses such as tactile, in feeling the grass or sand, or auditory, in hearing the trees blow or the roaring waves from the ocean. You can even help your child smell the scents of different kinds of flowers. The National Science Teachers Association (NSTA) supports exploratory play and active engagement for birth to age three.[7] It states, "At an early age, all children have the capacity and propensity to observe, explore, and discover the world around them" (NRC 2012).

18 months of age is also a time for the child to begin climbing on small slides or other enclosed park playground equipment. This develops **large motor**

skills and enhances confidence in the toddler for later climbing.

Prepare a child for a newborn baby coming into the family by telling him or her that he/she can be a good helper to the new sister or brother. This will help to alleviate jealousy toward the newborn baby.

As you remember to check the interest of the child, I would like to point out that every so often I notice a child is interested in a toy, yet avoids playing with it. If this happens I try to teach the child how to use the toy to determine the interest. For instance, I once had a two-year-old interested in a simple dog puzzle (see Chapter 4 *My First Chunky Puzzle Puppy Dog*) but was avoiding putting the puzzle pieces back because she had not been taught. Once I taught her how to place the dog puzzle pieces in the wood block, the toddler enjoyed doing puzzles because she now had the skills.

NOTES

1   Punkoney Sarah, (2012). Stacking Blocks and Math-
     ematicians, Stay at Home Educator.com

2   https://www.theedadvocate.org/sensory-science-
     connecting-childrens-science-learning-to-their-
     sensory-play/

3   Lillard, P. P., & Jessen, L. L. (2003). *Montessori from
     the Start*. New York: Schocken Books (pp 149–150)

4   Lillard, P. P., & Jessen, L. L. (2003). *Montessori from
     the Start*. New York: Schocken Books (pp 104)

5   Furth, Hans G., & Wachs, Harry. (1975). *Thinking
     Goes To School*, New York, Oxford University Press
     (pp 22, 23)

6   Lillard, P. P., & Jessen, L. L. (2003). *Montessori from
     the Start*. New York: Schocken Books (pp 86, 87,
     103)

7   https://static.nsta.org/pdfs/PositionStatement_
     EarlyChildhood.pdf

CHAPTER 4

Toys, Art, and Music at Two to Three and a Half Years

TOYS, ART, AND MUSIC AT TWO TO THREE AND A HALF YEARS

When presenting a toy to your child, remember to determine the interest. If the child plays with the toy, he/she is interested. If the child ignores it, he/she is not ready or interested. Give the child another toy of interest instead. Reintroduce the ignored toy two or three weeks later.

At this age, there are a couple of things you can do to motivate a toddler or child to play with a toy. First, if you are rotating the toys on the shelf about once every four days to once a week, this may stimulate the toddler to notice a different toy to choose and play with on his/her own. Second, I have discovered if you place a toy out where the child plays when he/she wakes up in the morning, or right after a nap, the child will usually play with that toy immediately. If the child does not play with the toy immediately, you can try another toy that may be of interest. The child may play with that same toy for three days. If so, don't change the toy out until you notice the toddler not playing with it. One does not want to overstimulate the toddler; yet one does not want the toddler to become bored of a toy either. As a reminder, do not place too many toys in front of the toddler or it may overstimulate the child, and he/she may not play with them.

 Simple puzzles made of wood such as *My First Chunky Puzzle Puppy Dog* by Melissa and Doug can be shown to the child at two years of age. However, a child may be ready to do a simple puzzle at 18 months. Once the child can place the puzzle pieces inside the puzzle correctly, then show the child how to place the puzzle pieces next to the puzzle on the right side and assemble it in the exact order. This teaches the important skills of visualization and copying, and it trains the eyes to track from left to right in preparation for reading. Simple wood puzzles can be purchased at Lakeshore Learning or at www.melissaanddoug.com.

 The child can begin playing with a geometric train made of wood called *Stacking Train Toddler Toy Ages 2-4*. Some toddlers are ready as early as 18 months with parental supervision. Others may not be ready until two and a half years of age. Each section should be worked separately at first. Then once the child can do all three sections separately, he/she can put all three sections together simultaneously. This train is very important for the skills of geometric shapes recognition, visualization, and fractions for later math. *The Stacking Train Toddler Toy* can be purchased at www.melissaanddoug.com.

 By now your child has listened to you sing children songs since birth. He/she is most likely singing along and has developed a sense of rhythm. For musical instruments, you want instruments that make real notes, not sounds. After the child has heard the real note several times, you can give a music symbol for it. I purchased a toy called *Little Hands Piano* at Lakeshore Learning that includes song note cards. I like this particular toy because the note sounds are easier on the ears. Make sure music toys don't harm the ears. Ages three to six.

Language at this age (usually between two and three years old) can be enriched by speaking to the child using adjectives, for example, "red car, yellow duck, and big green ball." As the toddler begins to understand adjectives, the parent or caregiver can begin to give directions using positional words "on, over, under, in front, behind." For instance, "Place the red car *on top* of the shelf."

PREREQUISITE FOR WRITING

 Geometric Demonstration Tray - a prerequisite for writing. This can be purchased at www. montessorioutlet.com. You may be able to find shapes similar to the *Demonstration Tray* at Lakeshore Learning or another store. Shapes should be taught before sounds and recognition of alphabet letters. The correct order of teaching **The Three** is (1) basic shapes, (2) alphabet letter sounds, and (3) recognition of or naming letters. You want to teach simple shapes, triangle, square, or rectangle, first because alphabet letters are made up of multiple and more complex shapes. For example, the child will see the triangle in the letter "A" before seeing the added detail. Please note, teaching **The Three** out of order can stress the vision system. Teaching academics too soon before the vision system is developed enough can stress the vision system also. Consequently, the child may become hyper and may incorrectly be labeled ADHD.

Say the name of the shape three times. Next, the child can finger trace the shape while saying the name of the shape simultaneously. This is called **sensory integration technique (also known as multisensory learning)**. The child sees the shape while touching and tracing it and says the name of the shape at the same time. This integrates the vision, tactile, and auditory senses. You can now ask the child to hand you the triangle (for example), or place the triangle in front of you to ensure he/she knows the name of the shape. Finally, ask the child the name of the shape. "What shape is this?" Usually a child is ready between two and a half to three years of age to finger trace and say the name of the shape. Again, determine the interest of the child for the Demonstration Tray.

 At two and a half years, give the child one colored pencil and a small piece of white paper for drawing. Note: Many educators are now suggesting to give your child a crayon and large paper to scribble at about 14 months old. For the two-and-a-half-year-old, you can take an 8-1/2 by 11 paper and cut it into quarters for the small paper. Colored pencils help the child develop hand dexterity because the pencils show shades of light and dark depending on how hard you press, unlike crayons. Crayons are usually too big for the child's hand too. If the child puts the pencil in his/her mouth, take it away and try another day.

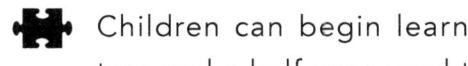 Children can begin learning colors between two and a half years and three years of age.

NOTE: There can be age variations on recognizing colors. Some children can recognize colors as early as 18 months. Others may not recognize colors until after age three.

The *Roll and Play* game stimulates color recognition beginning at about 18 months. It is also an excellent beginning game for teaching children to follow directions. Available at www.thinkfun.com/rollandplay.

The use of Montessori's *Cylinder Blocks* Parts 1 through 4 (https://montessorioutlet.com/authentic-montessori/sensorial.html) begin at age two and a half years. Children usually like the cylinders up through five years of age. It is a good idea to have two different types of *Cylinder Blocks* in your collection. That way two children can sit across a table from each other and each play with one. I chose this toy because it is self-correcting. This means the child can see the mistake and fix it on his/her own. A lot of the Montessori toys are self-correcting.

There are three ways to use the *Cylinder Blocks* from a beginning to a more advanced level. If you Google the internet, there are various ways to work the *Cylinder Blocks*. Make sure the largest cylinder is to the left. The first level is to show the child to take all the cylinders out and put them on the table. The child can now place the cylinders back into the correct holes. The second level is to place the cylinders about three to four feet away from the cylinder block. The child can now place each cylinder back into the correct holes. Finally, the third level is to place the cylinders around the room. Have the child go get each cylinder and place it back into the correct hole. Children enjoy these.

🧩 Nuts and bolts toys are good for **fine motor skills**.

🧩 The *Binomial Cube* can be shown to a child at three to three and a half years of age through the elementary years. The cube will help with the Binomial Theorem and the correct order for algebraic equations in later elementary school. Of course, the cube does not teach algebraic equations. This can be purchased at www.montessorioutlet.com. One can Google "How to Teach Montessori Binomial Cube." Then see Montessori Sensorial Lesson — Binomial Cube which you can view on YouTube. Hint: Take out all the cubes. Place the cubes that have a blue side facing up in a column. Place the cubes with a red side facing up in an adjacent column. Begin with the cube having all six red sides and place it on top of the picture lid. YouTube will show you the rest.

In my observation in a Montessori preschool classroom, and me teaching this cube in kindergarten, children do enjoy the *Binomial*

Cube. If you wish you can purchase and teach the child the *Trinomial Cube* once he/she masters the *Binomial Cube*. It is more advanced, but a preschooler or young elementary child who has mastered the *Binomial Cube* may enjoy the *Trinomial Cube* as well.

 Colored beads or cars can be strung which helps with **fine motor skills**. It is important to add some type of sewing to your collection of toys. I have chosen beads or cars to string because I have observed in a preschool classroom that children demonstrate a stronger interest in these than lacing cards. You can purchase a bucket of cars that includes lace at Lakeshore Learning. Ages three to six.

 Plastic Tweezers purchased at Lakeshore Learning can be used for transferring small colored erasers from bowl to bowl. Holding the tweezers is similar to holding a pencil (the three finger grasp—thumb, index, and middle finger), which will make the transition easier for writing. If the child is not interested in using the erasers, then you can purchase *Feed the Monkey* for transferring, from Lakeshore Learning.

Blocks or building sets, which are sometimes called Construction Manipulatives (term used by Lakeshore Learning), are very important for developing visualization and creativity skills. You may want to have seven or more different sets in your collection to rotate every four days or so for the child to build. The child may be interested in playing with these manipulatives through the elementary years.

AUDITORY ATTENTION AND CONCENTRATION

 The *Hearing* game or *Silence* game can be enjoyable for children from age three to six years. This builds attention and listening skills. Have your child or children lie down. Ask them to close their eyes. The parent or caregiver can move about clapping his/her hands, or tap on a table with an object such as a pencil in different parts of the room. The child/children can point to where the sound is coming from. One can also have the child/

children listen to different sounds in the room (e.g., feet shuffling, the door slamming, or wind blowing the blinds) and have them point in the direction every time they hear a sound in the room.

 Sound Boxes can be taught at age three and a half years as long as the child knows primary colors. This is important for deciphering different sounds and being able to match them. These sound boxes isolate the auditory sense and build concentration. Place all the red cylinders vertically in a column and all the blue cylinders vertically parallel next to the red cylinders. Have the child shake and listen to the sound of a red cylinder, for example, and then shake every blue cylinder to find the match of the sound from the red. Continue this process until each blue cylinder is matched to the red. This can be purchased from www. montessorioutlet.com.

 Simon Says is a good game for listening and following directions.

It will help the child focus if you look into his or her eyes as you speak.

CHAPTER 5

Language and Toys — Two and a Half to Six Years

LANGUAGE AND TOYS — AGES TWO AND A HALF TO SIX YEARS

- "Your baby must see you speaking so he can see, as well as hear, how words are pronounced."[1] Listen and respond to your baby's cues as well.

- Helping the child recall a special place such as the zoo or beach can enhance memory and language. At about two and half to three years old begin asking the child about these special places. For example, "What animals did you see at the zoo yesterday? What else did you do at the zoo?"

- Teach the child that loud voices are for outside, and quiet voices are for inside.

- Give the child a time frame when speaking about what you will do today, or tomorrow. Around the age of kindergarten or first grade before the child can tell time, you can say, for example, "Five minutes till dinner. Please clean up the toys."

- When picking up your child from preschool, ask him/her to tell you about his/her day. Usually the child will tell you everything about his/her day and may even sequence the day in order.

- Parents or caregivers should talk with short sentences. As a child understands short sentences, one can gradually add more words in a sentence when speaking.

- Rhyming books are important for reading.

- A child can match picture cards with items in a basket usually between ages three and four.

- *Spark Create Imagine Interactive Learning Plush Bear* — The bear sings familiar children's songs and tells stories. This can enhance language, auditory and listening skills. Available at Walmart.

- *Building Language Lotto* — for categorizing. Available at Lakeshore Learning.

- Play a naming game if the child is interested "What is this?"[2]

Positional Words Resource Box (purchase at Lakeshore Learning). These are words such as under, over, behind, in front of, etc. Or you can play a game at home using a car or other toy. Ask your child to place the car or toy over, under, behind, or in front of something. This helps in following directions. Then ask the question, "Is the car under, over, behind, or in front of something?" When the child answers the question, this develops language. The game can be played at about three and a half years old or earlier with parental supervision.

 Sequence Rummy using pictures can be purchased at Amazon and is very inexpensive. As you may recall the first steps in **sequencing** are order of dress and placing dishes on the shelf correctly. *Sequence Rummy* (these are cards) is the second step I use for **sequencing**, which will help for learning reading and writing. (Age three+) This is the beginning of placing pictures in the correct order and is a very important skill for reading comprehension such as recalling the beginning, middle, and end of a story. You can also purchase picture books without words and have the child tell you what is happening in each picture. In other words, you are having the child tell you a story.

Later on, one can use *Sequence Rummy* with the words on the back of the cards for **sequencing** in early reading.

 The third step in **sequencing** — When you read books to your child between ages five and six, practice reading very short stories. I recommend reading the story three times for comprehension. With your help, have the child tell you orally what the beginning of the story is about. Once the child can explain the beginning of the story (usually a few days to a week), then have the child describe the ending of the story. Lastly, have him/her describe the middle. Once the child can explain out loud each section from the book separately (the beginning, ending, and middle of the story), ask the child to explain the beginning, middle, and end of the story in sequence. As an experienced tutor, I highly recommend this skill be mastered by the end of first grade to enhance reading comprehension.

- *Zoob Car Designer* for building (available at Lakeshore Learning)

- *Marbulous* — the see-through one, which helps the child see the ball and track with the eyes. Tracking is good for reading and seeing a ball in movement (available at Lakeshore Learning). Children love this toy!

- Sorting or classifying household items and toys such as cars, animals, or building blocks and comparing, contrasting, adding, taking away, and noting similarities and differences can benefit children through age six. The higher level on classification involves questions on class inclusion. For example, "Are there more dogs, or more pets?"[3]

- *Color Tablets* (3rd box) I chose this box of color gradations tabs because I noticed the eyes must decipher detail when grading the colors. The child can pull any one chosen color tab out carefully with his/her thumb, index, and middle finger. Of course, this builds **fine motor skills**. It may take some time to be able to use these three fingers in pulling the tabs out and putting them back in the box. The child is asked not to touch the beautiful colored part of the tablet when taking each tab out of the box. Remind the child that the colors need to be placed back in the box in the exact same order. The color he/she chooses may be yellow, for example. Ask the child to place the yellow gradation tabs around the table not in graded order. Next, have the child grade the tabs from darkest to lightest vertically. I suggest to do one to two colors at a time to begin with. Once the child can grade many or all the colors from the box, he/she can place them all vertically around a yellow circle to make a sun. The parent or caregiver can cut out a large circle from yellow construction paper for the child to do gradations around the sun. Gradation of colors can begin between four and six years of age. The *Color Tablets* (3rd box) is available from www.montessorioutlet.com.

 Chutes and Ladders game — Ages 4+. This game is good for **directionality** (i.e., moving game pieces left to right, up and down). (Available at Target)

The best way for a child to learn a new language other than his/her own is to have someone else, who speaks the language fluently, converse with the child before age three.[4] In my tutoring experience, a child who is multilingual learns what I teach faster and comprehends better than those who speak only one language.

Anneliese's Schools (for people who live in Orange County, CA) teaches children ages two to sixth grade German, Spanish, and other languages. Each classroom usually focuses on a language every year depending on the bilingual teacher. A child may learn a second language nearly fluently by the end of the school year. My son was one of those children. You may be able to find a preschool in your area that also teaches languages beginning at age two. Otherwise, I recommend asking your preschool to bring in a teacher three times a week to teach the children another language.

NOTE: In my observation of children who are learning two languages such as English and Spanish beginning at birth, they may show signs of language delays. I am not usually alarmed by this because they are processing two languages. Many times I will see a rapid increase in language around age three and a half. Of course if you are concerned, you can always have your child seen by a Speech and Language Pathologist.

Regardless whether communicating in a first or second language, please ensure your caregiver speaks and writes complete sentences. This can make a difference in speech and language development.

THE NEXT STEPS FOR WRITING

 I recommend using sandpaper letters for the child to trace and learn the sounds of the letters. I suggest tracing three letters at a time. *Tactile Letters* are available at Lakeshore Learning.

Metal Insets — A child can begin tracing at age three or above if interested. This is the next step for writing after finger tracing. Use with three colored pencils. Children enjoy this activity. A box of 10 Insets are available at www.montessorioutlet.com.

 Learn To Print Practice Books — Books 1 and 2 (Age 4+). I am very impressed with these books. They teach left to right **directionality**. Remember in reading we read from left to right. The *Learn to Print Practice Books* also teach the proper letter formation. For **sensory integration**, one can copy the prewriting pattern onto a chalk board and have the child trace it with a different color chalk. This integrates the tactile, hearing, and vision senses because the child can hear the chalk across the board as he/she writes and sees the pattern simultaneously. Please make sure your child does not have an allergy to chalk. These books are available at Lakeshore Learning.

Anytime the child is willing to use a chalkboard, have him or her use it for **sensory integration**. The chalkboard is great for tracing and learning spelling words in elementary school.

Directionality involves learning left leg and arm, right leg and arm, etc. and should be taught in preschool. This is a very important developmental step that helps in alleviating letter reversals when the child begins to read or write. I am not concerned about a few letter reversals such as b's and d's or p's and q's up through second grade. However, if a student is reversing many letters in the last half of second grade, then I suggest seeing a Developmental Optometrist, F.C.O.V.D. (Fellow of the College of Optometrists in Vision Development). This type of Optometrist will be able to teach your student the proper steps in **directionality**. I once had a fourth grade student having many letter reversals in writing. She was having these issues because of missing the developmental step of learning her right and left sides of the body. Although I taught **directionality**, I sent this student to a developmental optometrist because she displayed other signs of vision deficiencies.

Playdates: I suggest playdates only be scheduled for less than two hours for toddler through first grade. You want playdates to be a positive experience for social development. After two hours, children can get tired, and it could result in a negative experience.

NOTE: The child is developing his/her social skills and self-esteem at preschool age. This needs to be fostered, which will help later on in life. I cannot stress enough to have a positive experience in preschool. Therefore, if a parent, teacher, or caregiver makes the child feel as though he/she is a bad kid, you may need to pull your child out of the situation. You can try to talk to the adult first in hopes of helping the adult make a change. But don't keep your child in a situation where social skills and self-esteem might be hindered by an adult for more than a few weeks.

Erik Erikson's Stage 3 — Purpose: Initiative versus Guilt — Ages 3–5.

Children who are treated warmly will try ideas. Children who are rejected may become inhibited and guilty. Children need to complete activities on their own for a purpose. Teachers or caregivers should be warmhearted and can help to support the child's efforts with proper choices.

TWO AREAS TO THINK ABOUT

First, different types of schools, whether public, private, Montessori,[5] or other have different benefits for each child. Public schools usually have a larger class size for learning, but may be beneficial to teach children social skills and to interact with others in large group settings. It may also help the children in being more well rounded (see under Important Points to Remember). Private schools can be beneficial in offering a smaller class size for learning. Montessori schools allow a child to go at his/her own pace and may help the child move ahead developmentally and academically. This type of school focuses more on the child's interest and is sensory oriented. Although, I am not going to go into detail any further regarding differences of schools because this is not the focus of my book, I am suggesting to research schools and do your best to choose a preschool or elementary school that fits your child's needs.

Second, since the focus of this book is primarily suggesting toys that enhance the senses, another area of development includes motor abilities, such as body balance or coordination of body axes. While many preschools may or may not be teaching this, a book called *Thinking Goes to School* by Hans G. Furth and Harry Wachs did a study called *The Charleston Project* at an elementary school that included teaching 24 general movement thinking games.[6] They state, "Many children perform academic tasks inadequately because they have not mastered the movement control on which these tasks depend." Parents may want to incorporate these general movement games in their child's play. In another study called *Perceptual-Motor Abilities and Prerequisites of Academic Skills*, motor persistence is tested by instructing a child to stand upright for 30 seconds (more detail in the study).[7] "Children with difficulties in maintaining body postures achieve considerably poorer results on all subtests which assess the abilities necessary for successful mastery of academic skills." Therefore, I did not want to leave out the importance of motor abilities in preparation for academic success.

AMAZING ATHLETES — SPORTS PROGRAM

Amazing Athletes[8] is a multisport program that teaches children from ages two and a half to six years

10 different sports such as tennis, baseball, football, and track and field. The program includes many ball sports and develops visual tracking and focusing related to **large motor skills**, such as throwing and catching. This enhances reading and writing in the classroom. Muscle tone helps with postural control, concentration and pen holding techniques. *Amazing Athletes* also promotes the following of directions and aids in counting and the identification of different ball sizes and colors. Ball skills also help to prevent nearsightedness. The *Amazing Athletes* program teaches children the correct placement of hands and feet for proper coordination. State or federal after-school programs may fund this activity. Otherwise, the *Amazing Athletes* program is very important to introduce to preschools. Parents may have to pay a fee. I recommend children attend two times a week to develop the skills this program offers.

If your school does not offer a program such as the *Amazing Athletes*, one can play throw and catch, or hit balls with your child.

IMPORTANT POINTS TO REMEMBER

It is important to remember to give the child an adequate amount of sensory toys and building block manipulatives through age six. Building blocks enhance visualization and help with math and language. Copying puzzles to the right also develops visualization as well as copying skills. Sorting or classifying helps with comparing or contrasting, similarities and differences, adding and taking away. According to Hans G. Furth and Harry Wachs in *Thinking Goes to School,* it takes a child about six years to have a mature class concept (higher level on classification).[9] After age six or seven, continue age appropriate manipulatives through age 11 or as long as the child is interested (see Chapter 6).

Remember the child notices shapes first before seeing details in letters. For example, the letter "A," which contains a triangle. The child must decipher the detail in the letter "A" after identifying the shape. Therefore, teach **The Three** in the correct order: Teach basic shapes, alphabet letter sounds, and finally recognition or name of the letters. It is best to only teach three letters at a time.

Rotating the toys on the shelf at least once a week (preferably mid-week) usually stimulates the child to choose a toy of interest. Placing a toy out after the child wakes in the morning or after a nap can also direct the child to manipulate that toy.

As you may recall from the introduction, this book is merely a guideline in preparation for academic success for your child, and the prevention of many learning disabilities. Each child is unique. What works for one child may not work for another in developing the senses. Determining the interest of the infant or child can help with readiness decisions.

I highly recommend reviewing each age group in this book as your child reaches that age for sensory development.

Please ensure your child has a healthy breakfast in the morning. In my observations and working in preschool and elementary classrooms, it makes a difference in the child's learning and focusing ability to stay on task when he/she has a nutritious breakfast. Honestly, I knew exactly which children in the preschool classroom did not have breakfast. It was much more difficult for them to focus. Of course, make sure your middle and high school student has breakfast as well. Additionally, it is always a good idea to talk about positive things at mealtimes.

The more routine provided, the more compliant the child will be.[10]

Enjoy observing your child's interests in activities.

Whether the toys are Montessori or from other toy stores I have discussed, many of these toys will develop fine motor skills and the five senses, enhance visualization for math and language, and build creativity. Large motor skills and visual tracking can be enhanced through a program such as the *Amazing Athletes*, or throwing and catching or hitting balls with your child. Social skills and self-esteem can be fostered when a child is treated warmly. All these areas of development can create a well rounded child, meaning the child can have strengths in many areas. This makes for a more confident child.

UNDERSTANDING HOW TO TEACH YOUR CHILD TO READ

I recommend the book *Overcoming Dyslexia*.[11] The author teaches the proper reading sequence for any child (dyslexic or not) to learn to read.

For first grade and older students, I discovered an excellent fluency technique by using Lakeshore Learning *Mini Rainbow Sentence Strips*. These colored paper sentence strips are 12 inches long and have lines for writing. Write or have the child write six words he/she already understands on one of the sentence strips using a black marker or pen. The words may come from a short story he/she is currently reading. Then have the child read the words very quickly. You may give your child new words on a new strip approximately every four days. The color helps the child retain the words, and saying the words quickly trains the eyes to track and read faster. This is one technique out of many I have used for tutoring first through fifth grade students.

When learning short and long vowel sounds in words, use workbooks that utilize both the word by itself and the word in a sentence. This way the child can transfer the single word to a sentence in reading or writing. I call this the **Transfer Technique**. An example would be the short "o" in the word "dog." The workbook should have a sentence for reading the word such as "The dog ran after the ball." If the workbook does not have a sentence for the short or long vowel word, then have your child write a sentence using the word "dog." If the child is unable to think of a sentence, you may have to provide one for the child to write.

Writing a sentence also transfers writing to reading. The child can then read the word and sentence three times.

In my experience beginning mid semester first grade, having your child or student read directions on worksheets aloud and asking the child to describe to you what he/she needs to do on the worksheet improves comprehension. For example: The child reads aloud "Say the name of the picture. Read the words. Draw a line from each word to the picture it names." You may need to explain to him/her there are three directions to follow. The child should say and explain the three directions to you and complete the worksheet in the exact order per the directions. In addition to improving comprehension, this technique also teaches the student sequencing and to answer all questions from the start.

Once your child is reading fluently (end of first grade or above), have your child read poems for rhythm and speed. I recommend your child read poems two times a week for six weeks.

NOTES

1   Lillard, P. P., & Jessen, L. L. (2003). *Montessori from the Start*. New York: Schocken Books (pp 170)

2   Lillard, P. P., & Jessen, L. L. (2003). *Montessori from the Start*. New York: Schocken Books (pp 172)

3   Furth, Hans G., & Wachs, Harry. (1975). *Thinking Goes To School*, New York, Oxford University Press (pp 16)

4   Montanaro, S. Q., M.D. (2007). *Understanding the Human Being*. Mountain View: Nienhuis Montessori USA (pp 144–147)

5   Use of Montessori in this book does not imply any affiliation with or endorsement by Montessori or its parent company.

6   Furth, Hans G., & Wachs, Harry. (1975). *Thinking Goes To School*, New York, Oxford University Press (pp 71)

7   Milica Gligorović et.al. (2011). *Perceptual-Motor Abilities and Prerequisites of Academic Skills* - https://scholar.Google.com/scholar?hl=en&as_sdt=0%2C5&q=perceptual+motor+abilities+and+prerequisites+of+academic&btnG= (pp 409, 414)

8   Henderson, J. (2010). Retrieved from *Amazing Athletes* - www.amazingathletes.com

9   Furth, Hans G., & Wachs, Harry. (1975). *Thinking
       Goes To School*, New York, Oxford University Press
       (pp 16)

10   Lillard, P. P., & Jessen, L. L. (2003). *Montessori from
       the Start*. New York: Schocken Books (pp 206)

11   Shaywitz, S., M.D. (2003). *Overcoming Dyslexia*.
       New York: Vintage Books

CHAPTER 6

Academic Success Tips for the Elementary Child

ACADEMIC SUCCESS TIPS FOR THE ELEMENTARY CHILD

TOYS AND TECHNIQUES

I have suggestions for sensory toys for the elementary student in helping him/her achieve higher level academic skills. Whether in public or private school, I have used these toys and the following techniques in tutoring with great success for more than 15 years on regular education students, and students labeled with a mild to moderate learning disability such as dyslexia, or the disability ADHD. With parental feedback and my own evaluation, I found most students see results both in the classroom and at home as early as three weeks. These skills usually only take two times a week for six to eight weeks to complete. (Note: I call this a Six Week Developmental Program. Some students, particularly fifth graders, may need eight weeks.) Most parents like to see speedy results in their child in higher level reading comprehension, writing and math skills, and even test scores in a short amount of time.

When I tutor, I use the sensory integration technique (see Chapter 4) whenever possible. This way if a student has a weak sense, the other strong senses help the student learn. The weak sense can also be strengthened through this technique.

If a public or private school has an intervention specialist or special education teacher on staff, the teacher may want to use these sensory toys or techniques for a student to overcome obstacles in learning.

 One of the most important games I suggest to add to your collection of toys for sensory integration and speed is the *Bop It! XT* or *Bop It! Extreme* game. Keep a student chart for six weeks and have the child play this game two or more times a week to improve his/her score. Through experience I discovered that when a student reaches a score of 25 or more, an academic growth spurt occurs. I usually use this game for second grade on up. Fifth graders love this game as well as many adults. Check online for availability.

Tangrams called *Playful Patterns* help in memorization of math facts and other math concepts, visualization, and language. When students have used the tangrams and other manipulatives correctly at an early age, they appear to learn math concepts quicker in middle or high school. In using *Playful Patterns* for visualization, ask the child to copy the picture card by placing the shapes to the right of the card. Make sure to have the child say the name of the shape as he/she pulls the shape out of the box (See the **sensory integration technique**, Chapter 4). Choose only four to five cards at a time. Have your child play the game two times a week until the cards are completed. It usually takes three to four weeks. As a tutor I used the *Playful Patterns* on grades K–5. *Playful Patterns* is available at Discovery Toys or Amazon.

Once the Tangram cards are completed, one can teach the child to flip the large right triangle from the *Playful Patterns*. First begin with flipping one direction. Start with the right angle of the right triangle pointed toward the right. Then ask the child to show you what the triangle will look like if flipped to the left (you may have to demonstrate this). The child should flip the triangle to the left. You can now say, "What will the triangle look like flipped down?" The child will most likely say "the same." Now say, "What will the triangle look like flipped up?" Again, the child will probably say "the same." Next say, "What will the triangle look like flipped to the right?" The child should show the placing of the right angle of the triangle pointed to the right. Once the child can follow directions flipping the triangle one direction at a time (this may only take one session), you can now give him/her multiple directional moves at the same time. For example, "What does the triangle look like when it is flipped to the left and down?" Now say, "What does the triangle look like when it is flipped up and to the right?" "What does the triangle look like when it is flipped up and then down?" Then continue the process with two directional moves. The child has to visualize the final position of the triangle after completing the two directional moves and then places the triangle in the final position. Lastly, once the child can flip the triangle mentally in two directional moves, ask the child to show you what the triangle looks like after three directional moves when flipped. For example, "left, down, and to the right," or "up, down, and to the left," and so on. Visualizing the final position of the right triangle after two and three directional moves could take about four sessions of practice.

NOTE: If the child confuses the left and right on the triangle, he/she may need to learn directionality from a developmental optometrist.

 Geoboards with pattern cards and rubber bands. I usually place this toy in front of the student to occupy him/her while I prepare to tutor. I have the student begin with the easiest pattern card and build up each session to a more difficult pattern. The latter patterns usually require multiple rubber bands. In copying the pattern, the student needs to place the rubber band on the exact pegs as shown on the card. This enhances fine motor skills and eye-hand coordination, copying, plane geometry or other math skills, and spatial relations. I use this technique for first through fifth grade.

Some students may be ready before this age. *6 Pack Double-Sided Geoboard Mathematical Manipulative Material Array Block Geo Board* is available at Amazon. Lakeshore Learning sells a packet of plastic colorful *Geoboards* if extras are needed.

 Pre-K Visual Discrimination Printables - Through learning similarities and differences in these printable cards, the eyes decipher details. This can help in seeing the differences in p's and q's, and b's and d's. I use visual discrimination cards for pre-K to fifth grade such as the *Gingerbread Matching cards* and *Three Billy Goats Gruff Visual Discrimination cards*. You can print the cards at www. prekinders.com.

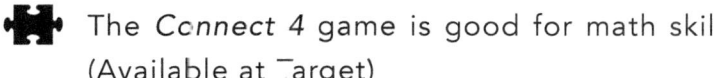 The *Connect 4* game is good for math skills. (Available at Target)

If the elementary student is interested in any building kits through age 11, I highly recommend them.

I have discovered that in using these toys and techniques (especially the Tangrams), I do not usually need to teach math problems to students in grades

K–4. However, I find most fifth grade students do benefit from doing some math problems once they have completed the Tangrams. If the fifth grade student is ready, I like to work on decimals beginning with place value, and then rounding, addition, subtraction, and multiplication. If the student is not ready, usually a review of addition, subtraction, multiplication and division with whole numbers works well. And if time permits, I will tutor in fractions. I only teach five to eight math problems per session so the student does not tire easily. Five problems may be a new concept taught for three sessions. The other three problems are a review from the day or week before.

THE STUDENT STRUGGLING IN READING COMPREHENSION

For a student struggling in reading comprehension who cannot repeat back to you the beginning, middle, or ending of the story, please refer back to Chapter 5, the third step in **sequencing** to teach this skill. However, instead of reading short stories to your child, have your child read to you. He/she should read the story three times. The first is for sounding out new words (try to avoid too many new words in a story) and reading the story out loud. The second is for fluency of the new words and reading out loud. Finally, the third time through is for reading silently. The student will have to take a test from reading silently in the elementary years. Reading three times helps the student comprehend the beginning, middle, and ending of the story. It also improves test taking skills for answering questions about the story. These test questions may ask the main idea of the story, the description of the character (e.g., Is the character, nice, helpful, or greedy?), or what happened first in the story. Once the student can comprehend well and answer test questions correctly, you only need to have the student read the story twice, once aloud, once silently.

In about third grade students may be taking tests that ask for more than one sub-question to be answered in one test question. It could be on a history or a science test. For example, Question #5 - "How many planets are in our solar system?" "What is the largest planet?" "Which planet is the farthest away?" In my tutoring experience, students may not know to answer all the sub-questions in Question #5 and end up with a lower grade. Teachers can teach students in the classroom before taking the test to answer all of the test questions. Parents can teach their child at home to answer all questions for homework. Once the student is familiar with this type of question, he/she should be independent in answering all questions.

THE STUDENT STRUGGLING IN WRITING

There is a **Descriptive Writing Technique** I use with great success for the elementary student who cannot express words on paper (or typed on a computer keyboard). One can help the student do this technique two times a week for four to six weeks. Through experience in tutoring the elementary student, I discovered that only describing orally does not always transfer over to paper. Therefore, I integrated describing orally with written description. I use the following technique for grades second and higher, although I have used this on some first graders.

Place a pencil and one sheet of unlined letter size paper in front of the student. I use unlined paper to help the student express descriptive language without the worry of staying in the lines. Writing on paper also enhances brain activity instead of a Tablet.[1] Later on (see week 3 for descriptive writing), the student will use college-ruled paper. The proper order for descriptive writing is:

1. Ask the student to describe a pencil orally. One can give him/her an example for the first time in describing. "Is the pencil long?" "What color is the pencil?" Finally, "What can you do with a pencil?" After the student describes the pencil verbally, then ask him/her to describe the pencil in writing. The student may not write exactly what he/she described verbally. That is okay. See examples in Appendix A. He or she may only write one or two sentences. Now ask the student to read his/her sentences aloud and look for any errors to correct. The errors could be a missing punctuation mark, missing capitalization, or a spelling error.

2. Next ask the student to look for any duplicated beginning words in consecutive sentences. The words may be the word "the" followed by the word "the" in the next sentence. For example, "The pencil is long. The pencil is yellow." Now ask the student

to change one of the words at the beginning of the second sentence to another word at the beginning of the sentence. For instance, since the first sentence states "The pencil," the second sentence could be worded "It is yellow." Explain to the student that a sentence should begin with a different word to avoid repetition.

3. Now have the student write a final sentence, and rewrite all the sentences with the corrected version.

4. Finally ask the student to re-read the corrected version out loud.

The purpose of descriptive writing is to help the student visualize objects, events, or situations so they may be described verbally or in writing. As the student practices descriptive writing twice a week, the writing will increase in length. See Appendix A.

The following is a suggested list of words for second and third graders to use at the beginning of a sentence: *Also, Most, Now, Some, Sometimes,* or *Then.*

This is a suggested list of advanced and transitional words for fifth grade and higher to use at the beginning of sentences: *Therefore, However, Although, Fortunately,* or *Moreover.*

Here is the proper progression for the **Descriptive Writing Technique**:

Week 1   Two times a week describe an object such as a pencil, apple, or candle.

NOTE: After the student describes an object orally (e.g., apple), take the apple away while the student writes the description on paper. This improves visual memory.

Week 2   Two times a week describe something other than an object such as a classroom wall or a wall at home.

Week 3   Two times a week ask the student to read a short passage that describes something such as a car, animal, or insect. Have the student say the description out loud. Then write the description on college-ruled paper.

Follow the order (1–4) above for descriptive writing.

SHORT MATH CLASSES — SUMMERTIME

For continued confidence in math, Saddleback College in Mission Viejo, CA, offers two week math classes during summer session under the category College for Kids for fourth grade and up. The classes are challenging. Therefore, your child will only learn what he/she is developmentally capable of learning. Don't be alarmed by this challenge because he/she will learn more than you expect. The student will usually be confident in math from the very first week of school beginning in the fall. If your child is lacking math skills, these summer classes can enhance math skills for this type of student as well. There may be other junior colleges or facilities that offer two-week math courses during summertime for continued student confidence.

ADDITIONAL HELPFUL TIPS

 To alleviate eye strain and not break a student's concentration, I recommend having the student take a break after the academic or computer activity is completed. The child can stand up, look around and look out the window. If the child appears fidgety, such as pulling on his/her shirt or moving in his/her chair, or shows signs of watery eyes, I have him/her take a break before the activity is completed. One has to find the correct balance in not interrupting the student's concentration and alleviating eye strain.

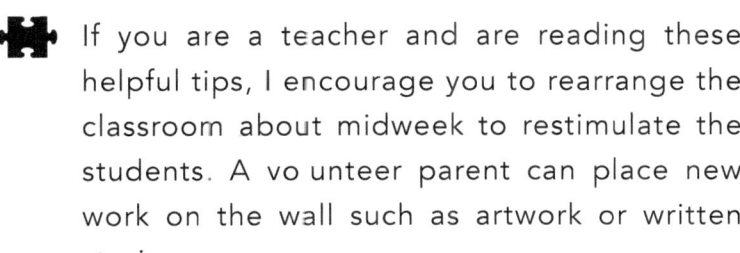 If you are a teacher and are reading these helpful tips, I encourage you to rearrange the classroom about midweek to restimulate the students. A volunteer parent can place new work on the wall such as artwork or written stories.

If a child does not have a proper desk and chair to do homework, I suggest purchasing the *Posture-Rite Lap Desk*. You can also use this desk in the car. The lap desk ensures eyes are at the proper distance and promotes good posture. The *Posture-Rite Lap Desk* is available at www.amazon.com. Walmart may carry this desk as well.

As a tutor, I evaluate my students every day and ask myself, "What is working; what is not working?" This is called **self-reflection**. For example, my second grade student was very good at subtracting two-digit numbers. However, this student was unable to read words containing short vowels. So I created worksheets with sentences using short vowel words. Usually I teach a new skill three times to ensure the student has mastered it and then review periodically.

 I recommend the older elementary child (fourth grade and higher) use a checklist worksheet to assess the completion of tasks. The parent or child can request this from the teacher, if not already provided, or create one. This worksheet could be used to ensure that the contents of a California Missions report are complete, for example. The checklist could include rows for name, date, title page, table of contents, introduction, specific information on each mission, and a conclusion. The older elementary child will check off each section when it is completed. This will ensure the student avoids incomplete work and will improve his/her grade.

Every child has a skill or talent that he/she can develop. When I tutored, I would look for that special talent each student exhibited. One of my fifth grade students had an exceptional ability in drawing. I suggested the parent have him consider attending an art school. Focusing on a student's special talent may help prevent boredom, depression, or use of alcohol/drugs later on.

Erik Erikson's Psychosocial Development Stage 4 — Competency: Industry versus Inferiority — Ages 5–12 years.

This is the period for children to discover their interests. This is the age range for enrichment opportunities. The child begins to realize what he/she is good at such as a ball sport, a musical instrument, drawing, dance, singing, a technical skill, etc. Children realizing their interests and talents and being allowed to develop them at this age may be more motivated and have higher self-esteem. This is also a vital period for self-confidence. It is important for students to do well in school so they feel good about themselves. Peer acceptance is significant at this stage. Students should be productive to complete work and meet teacher's and parent's expectations. Teachers, parents, or caregivers should praise students for their work. This will help the students to be diligent. If one ridicules students, they can feel inferior.

All these sensory toys, techniques, and helpful tips have motivated many elementary students to become more independent, productive, successful, and confident in the classroom and at home.

CONCLUDING REMARKS: OBSERVATIONS, BENEFITS, AND DISCOVERIES

I have observed in teaching the proper use of these sensory toys and techniques for the elementary student that they appear to enhance the visual, auditory, and tactile senses. These tools promote academic success. A study with the help of a Developmental Optometrist or Auditory Specialist may confirm enhancement of the visual and auditory senses.

Upon completing a six to eight week program utilizing these tools, several students who were borderline special education or labeled with a mild to moderate learning disability such as dyslexia, or the disability ADHD qualified for the Gifted and Talented Education GATE program. Interestingly, in observing GATE students, I noticed their senses seem to be more developed.

In my experience, some of the benefits of this program include children being promoted to the next grade, students qualifying for the GATE program, and the child becoming more independent and confident. Children also become more social because of their competence academically. Parents are more confident in raising their child because of this knowledge in sensory development or other skills. I have seen positive changes in families after their child has received these tutoring techniques.

Also noteworthy, ironically, I discovered that virtually every student I tutored, whether in public or private school in a time span of 15 years, was deficient in sequencing for reading, fine motor skills, and visualization for writing and math. It appeared these students were not prepared via sensory development for academic success. This may be due to a lack of sensory development or perceptual-motor ability education classes for parents and teachers.

In the study *Perceptual-Motor Abilities and Pre-requisites of Academic Skills*, for 1,165 children ages 7½–11 from Belgrade, "Results clearly indicate the importance of perceptual-motor functions in the development of the abilities which are prerequisites of academic skills."[2]

The study *Postural Variability and Sensorimotor Development in Infancy* states, "Visual attention combined with active experiences contacting the object advances the development of reaching more than passive interactions or only visualizing the object.[3] Taking together, these examples suggest that those infants who have had active movement experiences have the ability to perceive visual and tactile stimuli, and modify postural control and reaching strategies in response to the task demands during the first months of life." The conclusion states, "While further research is needed, the basic science, theoretical approaches, and measurement of postural complexity during development all suggest the importance of movement, and sensory experience in early development." This suggests to me that the early experience of placing the Boomering in the infant's hand may help with a child's motor abilities, his/her sensory development, and some prerequisites for academic success from the *Perceptual-Motor*

Abilities study. More research from infancy through kindergarten may be required.

I hope these studies and my presentation in this book give parents or caregivers knowledge so that children will be better prepared academically, and/or be able to overcome obstacles they may encounter.

NOTES

1   Neuroscience News. University of Tokyo,
     (March 19, 2021). Stronger Brain Activity After
     Writing on Paper Than Tablet or Smartphone.
     www.neurosciencenews.com

2   Milica Gligorovic et.al. (2011). *Perceptual-Motor
     Abilities and Prerequisites of Academic Skills*
     - https://scholar.Google.com/scholar?hl=en&as_
     sdt=0%2C5&q=perceptual+motor+abilities+
     and+prerequisites+of+academic&btnG= (pp 424)

3   Dusing, Stacey C. (March 29 2016). *Postural Vari-
     ability and Sensorimotor Development In Infancy*
     - Developmental Medicine and Child Neurology
     - www.onlinelibrary.wiley.com

CHAPTER 7

Warning Signs

WARNING SIGNS

VISION DEFICIENCIES

Beginning in the second grade, be aware of some of these possible vision deficiencies:

- A child does not stay on task to complete schoolwork in a timely manner.

- A student skips lines or words when reading.

- The student loses his/her place when reading.

- He/she has difficulty copying from the classroom board.

- The student is too close to the page when reading or writing.

Have your child's eyes checked for reading glasses in the second grade through a Developmental Optometrist (F.C.O.V.D.) if you suspect some of these issues. I have seen miraculous improvement when a second grader low in vision development was prescribed reading glasses. The optometrist may also suggest a Vision Training Program if the reading glasses are not sufficient to promote the vision skills. The optometrist should teach visualization as well. For optimal results, the student should have a tutor for academics, be taught visualization skills, and be enrolled in a vision training program simultaneously.

For more information on vision problems, refer to the book *The Mislabeled Child.*[1]

STRATEGIES TO HELP PREVENT NEARSIGHTEDNESS

- Balls skills (Amazing Athletics, or any type of ball sports)

- Make sure the child's face is not too close to his surface when reading or writing. Also, the child should not get too close when using a computer or other electronic devices (such as a cell phone or iPad, etc.). Desk height should be at about the belly button. One can also change the chair height.

Monitor the print size on worksheets, making sure the print is large, especially in grades K–2. I once observed a teacher give a first grade classroom worksheets that used a font size for third graders. About half of the class was off task due to the print being too small.

 The child can look around the classroom and look outside a window after an activity is completed. See information regarding eye strain under Additional Helpful Tips in Chapter 6.

 When transitioning from large to small print (usually in the fourth grade), have the child switch back and forth from large to small, and small to large, to help the eyes adjust to smaller print. One can request the teacher create worksheets in different size fonts to help the child's eyes transition better. If there is not an adjustment period to small print, this may create vision problems. Of course it is always less stressful on the eyes to read larger print.[2]

AUDITORY IMPAIRMENTS

There are two types of auditory impairments. The first is hearing loss, and the second is Central Auditory Processing Deficit (CAPD).[3]

Examples of possible auditory hearing loss:

- Lacks response to voices or loud noises.

- Inability to understand what is said.

- Repeatedly asking "What?"

- Difficulty hearing indoors compared to outdoors.

- When talking to a child, he/she confuses beginning sounds. For example, he mistakes "dad" for "bad," thinking you said "bad" to him when you were actually talking about his dad.

The test for hearing loss is called audiometric tone detection test.

Some examples of Central Auditory Processing Deficits are:

- The child may be unable to hear in the presence of background noise.

- Lacks auditory memory.

- Mishearing words (i.e., words sound alike to a child with CAPD).

- Unable to tell where sounds are coming from.

- Sound hypersensitivities such as when a child can hear too much of a certain sound. He/she can become distracted or perhaps aggressive and can be incorrectly labeled ADHD.

Some Auditory Attention behaviors are:

- A child loses attention when a teacher reads or talks too long.

- The child may daydream or appear spacey.

- He/she may have difficulty following oral directions.

Accommodations in the classroom may include:

- Seating the child close to the teacher where he/she can see the teacher speaking.

- Seating the child away from noises such as a fan blowing or a noisy heater.

- Seating the student next to a quiet student.

The test for CAPD is a full range Central Auditory Processing (CAP) test. Make sure the CAP test is not the SCAN-C test which is limited for CAPD. One can find more information and the list of CAPDs in the book *The Mislabeled Child*.

If you suspect an auditory impairment, please be sure and check both hearing loss and Central Auditory Processing with a specialist. Autistic children should be checked once a year. Please note, it can be difficult to test children under the age of five. Therefore, if you suspect an auditory impairment, test your child every year.

NOTES

1   Eide, Brock M.D., M.A., & Eide, Fernette M.D.
     (2006). *The Mislabeled Child*, New York, Hyperion
     Books (pp 73, 76)

2   Fashion Eyeglass World. (January 7, 2017). *Why It's
     Better to Read Large Print Books* - www.fashioneye-
     glassworld.com

3   Eide, Brock M.D., M.A., & Eide, Fernette M.D.
     (2006). *The Mislabeled Child*, New York, Hyperion
     Books (pp 112, 114, 118, 119, 131, 152)

CHAPTER 8

Keeping Your Adolescent Focused

KEEPING YOUR ADOLESCENT FOCUSED

MIDDLE AND HIGH SCHOOL

At about seventh to eighth grade one can begin to teach advanced vocabulary words. When advanced words are introduced, I suggest using the word in sentences and passages. This promotes an understanding of the word's definition and helps to prepare your adolescent for high school and college. There may be summertime classes that teach this skill. In addition to learning higher-level words, your adolescent may continue to take short math classes in the summertime for confidence through ninth or tenth grade.

Once your adolescent finds an interest, encourage him/her to continue with that interest. This could be a sport, a musical instrument, church youth group involvement, holding an office such as school president, singing in a choir, or being involved in a club activity. Keeping your adolescent focused on interests may keep him/her from getting into mischief.

COLLEGE AGE

College can be an easy transition from high school. Sometimes, however, it can be difficult. Sadly, I have observed that some adolescents free of drugs in high school began using drugs in college. Since the brain is still developing until about age 25, adolescents may not always make the wisest decisions. For that reason and some others, a group of adolescent health experts suggest adolescence extend to age 24.[1] Understanding this, parents may be able to keep the communication open with their adult child. You may be able to help the child stay focused on his/her interest or career path.

The following are suggestions for communicating with your adult child:

- Talk about his/her continued interest or talent.

- Discuss classes for his/her career path.

- Let your adult child know what you agree with and what you don't agree with.

- Have a significant other person in your adult child's life, such as a grandparent, to reinforce your beliefs.

This may help your adolescent through the college-age years and help you stay connected with him/her later on in life. His/her amazing skills or talents can help make a difference in the working world.

NOTES

1   Miller, Korir. (January 19, 2018). *Adulthood Now Begins At Age 24*, Say Scientists - www.yahoo.com

I truly wish your child the best in academic success and achieving his/her every dream.

Acknowledgments

Dr. Steven Cohn, O.D., F.C.O.V.D., for his expertise in the proper visualization steps and directionality.

R. J. Kost, Curriculum Coordinator, for his advice and curriculum specialties.

Dean Gilbert, Science/STEM Consultant, EDU Consulting LLC, for his science expertise.

Jillian Harvey, my editor, for making this book better.

Irena H., for her support and gratefulness in tutoring her girls, and use of some work samples.

My mother, Darlene, for her editing suggestions.

My loving husband, David, for his assistance.

APPENDIX A

Descriptive Writing Samples

Descriptive Writing Samples
Demonstrating Rachel's Progression
(Third Grade)

1-12-10   (Rachel

I'm going to discribe my pincel, it's black
it's sharpend, it has a eraser, the
eraser is raped in metle, and
has words on

I'm going to discribe my pencil. It's
black and Sharpend. It has one eraser and
the eraser is raped in metl. The
pencil has words on it. Pencils are
used for writing.

Descriptive Writing Samples
Demonstrating Rachel's Progression

Rachel 1-26-10

My Apple

My apple is lopsided. (No) It is a red apple.

Also, it has no stem and it's denten. Apples are very helthy for you to eat.

My mom's office   Rachel
                                   2-8-10

My mom's office is red, filled with papers, and very busy.

My mom work

Descriptive Writing Samples
Demonstrating Rachel's Progression

Rachel
2-16-10

My living room

My living room is shaped
like a rectangle and has
lots and lots of pictures.
The sopha is dark brown and the
tv is 52 inches. There are about
30 magizens and 1 fire place.
The fire place is made of metle
and is good for cold winter
days. I also have a coffee table
There is one tishue box on it.
In the living room there is
confedy carpet. My confedy
carpet is light brown. I love
my living room.

Descriptive Writing Samples
Demonstrating Rachel's Progression

Rachel
2-23-10

Spider

I hate spiders. There hairy little creatchers and I don't like them. I exashly don't like the big ones. Thse big ones creep me out. I really hate spiders (Oh theirs one right next to me! Oh wait no there isn't. It was Just me. So as I was saying, the tarentula is a disgusting animal to me. Because I have seen alot of movies with killer spiders.

3-2-10 Take my advice don't ever watch spider movie's! With their bent legs that look like bent coat hangers. And theres eight of them with black toes at the botm of each leg. It is to scary. I think spider movies are awful.

Descriptive Writing Samples
Demonstrating Rachel's Progression

Model - Car   3-9-10
                      Rachel

My model car is red and smooth. The
front comes to a point witch makes
it go faster. It also has a lighting
bult on the sides. Before they detalled
the car they had to' pule off bottle capps
and the end. They took off the
end because it was too heavy.
This model - car is my favorite

Descriptive Writing Samples
Demonstrating Rachel's Progression

Rachel
3-16-10

Moon Cakes

A moon cake is a cake that Chinese people like to eat. The moon cake is very disgusting to me, but alot of chinese people say it is good. The moon cake is made of black beans, fruit, egg yolk, seeds and nuts. You can find moon cakes in many stors. But some people like to make their own moon cakes. You may only find moon cakes in china.

Descriptive Writing Samples
Demonstrating Rachel's Progression

Rachel
3-23-10

Whales

Whales are mammals. They come in many different sizes and shapes. Also, most whales come in different colors such as white, gray, or black. Most whales have one blowhole, but some have two. A blowhole is what a whale breeths out of. Some whales can grow up to 4 feet and some can grow up to 100 feet. Whales are a very interesting animal!

Descriptive Writing Samples
Demonstrating Rachel's Progression

Baskets   Rachel
                           3-29-6

Most baskets are made of plants.
Baskets are very hard to make. In order to
make a basket you need rope. Some baskets
are made of sticks, twigs, and treebark. Most
baskets are plain but some have dye. Dye is
colors, that make your basket look neat.
Many peoplts use baskets to heild things.
And some are used for jobs and many other
things too. Lastly my grandma makes baskets
too.

Descriptive Writing Samples
Demonstrating Elyse's Progression
(Second Grade)

Elyse

1—10

The Pencil has a pink eraser. The (led) is (poyntey) The wood is tan (arord) the (led) There is black printing. The Pencil is yellowish. The Pencil is in use is black printing to (rite) words.

Descriptive Writing Samples
Demonstrating Elyse's Progression

Elyse   1-19-10

The lemon is yellow. it has skraches on it. It is bad. It is a cerkel. A lemon is used for a Pie.

The lemon is yellow. It has scrathes on it. The lemon is bad. It is a circle. A lemon is used for a pic.

Descriptive Writing Samples
Demonstrating Elyse's Progression

Elyse 1-26-10

My (appel) is red, yellow, and orange.
It is shaped like a olval. The (appel) can role.
You can play (kech) with it. I cane eat
the (appel) too.

Descriptive Writing Samples
Demonstrating Elyse's Progression

Elyse   2-2-10

I The   It's It You Also Next then
firally lastly

The candel is redish. It is hard. It's from costco.

They are sitting on a candel holder. Finally,
you can hert your hand if you tuch the
waks.

Elyse   2-9-10

My mom's ofis is derteyred. It is squar.

There x are chares. I have a sockerbal
in the ofis. A computer is on her desk.
Lastly, my momy does her work in there!

Descriptive Writing Samples
Demonstrating Elyse's Progression

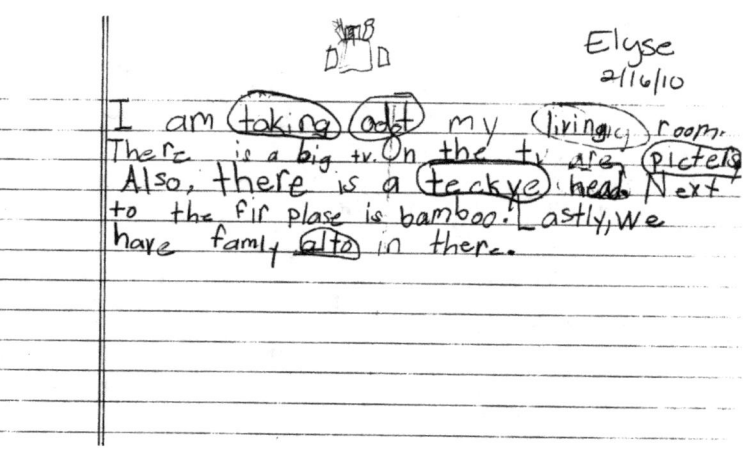

Elyse
2/16/10

I am (taking) (odt) my (living) room. There is a big tv. On the tv are (picters) Also, there is a (teckye) head. Next to the fir plase is bamboo. Lastly, we have famly (alto) in there.

Descriptive Writing Samples
Demonstrating Elyse's Progression

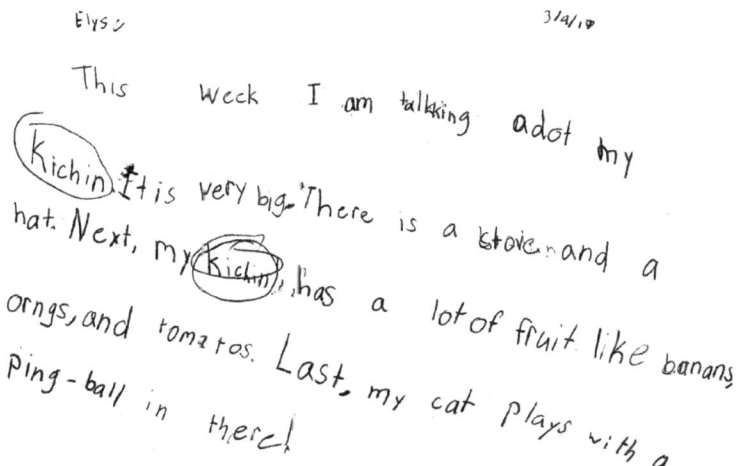

Descriptive Writing Samples
Demonstrating Elyse's Progression

5-23-10   Elyse

At a moon cake festival there are First, they make very gross moon cakes. These are the ingredons black beans, seed, nunt, fruit, or even an egg yolk. Next, they are shaped like a family in a circle. Then, they do this for the Chinese. Last, they sel them at the bakeries. That is what I leaned adout moon cakes.

alot of food.

Places to Purchase Sensory Toys

PLACES TO PURCHASE SENSORY TOYS

- Amazon
  www.amazon.com

- buybuyBaby
  www.buybuybaby.com

- Discovery Toys
  www.discoverytoys.com

- Fisher-Price
  www.fisherprice.com

- HABA Toys
  www.habausa.com

- Lakeshore Learning
  www.lakeshorelearning.com
  discount coupons through e-mail or text

- Melissa and Doug Toys
  www.melissaanddoug.com

- Montessori Toys
  www.montessorioutlet.com
  online discount store (toys are generally discounted 50% or more)

- Other Educational Items (e.g., children's kitchen utensils)
  www.montessoriservices.com

- Skyflight Mobiles
  www.hangingmobilegallery.com

- Target Stores
  www.target.com

- Walmart
  www.walmart.com

- Wee Gallery
  www.weegallery.com

ABOUT THE AUTHOR

Terri Hadley was a tutor for regular education, special needs, and at-risk students for more than 15 years. She specialized in sensory integration and development for academic success. Having a Bachelor of Science degree in Child and Adolescent Development helped Terri understand the theories for age appropriate learning. Terri also lectured on Sensory Development — Preparing Your Child for Academic Success — Newborn to Age Six. Her goal as a tutor was to help the student be confident, independent, and successful in the classroom. She achieved this reward many times throughout the 15 plus years of tutoring including having several students test into the Gifted and Talented Education Program (GATE). Terri decided to turn her lecture into a book because parents have said they wished there was a class like this on Sensory Development to prepare their child academically. Therefore, Terri wants to spread sensory development information worldwide to help parents, grandparents, and caregivers prepare their child for academic success.